Anger Management God's Way

Daniel C. Okpara

Bible Ways to Control Your Emotions, Get Healed of Hurts and Respond to Offenses

..Plus Powerful Daily Prayers to Overcome Bad Anger Permanently

Disclaimer

The information presented herein represents the views of the author as of the date of publication. Because of the rate with which conditions change, the author reserves the rights to alter and update his opinions based on the new conditions. This product is for spiritual edification, bible study and informational purposes only and the author does not accept any responsibilities for any liabilities resulting from the use of this information.

While every attempt has been made to verify the information provided here, the author and his referrals cannot assume any responsibility for errors, inaccuracies or omissions. If there are any slights of people or organizations, please note that they are unintentional and are highly regretted.

Copyright © July 2017 by Daniel C Okpara

All Rights Reserved. Contents of this book may not be reproduced in any way or by any means without written consent of the publisher, with exception of brief excerpts in critical reviews, bible study and articles.

Published By:
Better Life Media.
BETTER LIFE WORLD OUTREACH CENTER.
Website: www.BetterLifeWorld.org
Email: info@betterlifeworld.org

Any scripture quotation in this book is taken from the KJV except where stated. Used by permission.

All texts, calls, letters, testimonies and enquiries are welcome.

Dedication

I dedicate this book to my wife, Doris Ngozi Okpara. She is the beautiful angel that God sent to come and package my life and make me a better person.

Table of Contents

Disclaimer..3

FREE BONUS 8

Introduction: Don't Manage Anger, Deal With It.................9

Chapter 1: Meaning and Types of Anger.............................15

Chapter 2: The Spirit of Anger..34

Chapter 3: Causes (and Sources) of Anger..........................43

Chapter 4: The Dangers of Anger...60

Chapter 5: How to Deal With Anger.....................................67

Chapter 6: Dealing With Anger Through Prayers...............90

Prayer 1: A Prayer of Confession and Total Surrender.........96

Prayer 2: Power to Exercise Forgiveness Now and Every Day...107

Prayer 3: Surrender Your Right to Be Angry.....................120

Prayer 4: Bind the Spirit of Anger..........................127

Prayer 5: Manifesting the Fruits of the Holy Spirit..........142

Prayer 6: Prayer for Those Who Struggle With Anger........149

Prayer 7: Declare the Promises of God For Your Life and Family..157

Other Books from The Same Authors................................170

Contact Us...174

About The Author...175

FREE BONUS ...

Download These 4 Powerful Books Today for FREE... And Take Your Relationship With God to a New Level.

www.betterlifeworld.org/grow/

Introduction: Don't Manage Anger, Deal With It

"Learn this from me. Holding anger is a poison. It eats you from inside. We think that hating is a weapon that attacks the person who harmed us. But hatred is a curved blade. And the harm we do, we do to ourselves" - Mitch Albom

Anger is one of the most powerful, destructive, and harmful emotions that we can experience. If not dealt with in the proper way, it can have severe life-changing consequences.

Pressures of work, family or others' wrong-doing are

some things that can cause anger. When not resolved, anger creates a vigorous desire to destroy something.

A man came back from work one day and suddenly became angry with his wife who was not yet back from work. His anger degenerated to bitterness when he saw his wife alighting from a vehicle of the man that brought her home. When the wife entered the house, he asked her about the man that brought her home. In an utter amazement she responded "your uncle of course". This is not the first time his uncle had brought her home.

He took his phone and called his uncle to confirm what the wife told him, and the uncle who never expected the man to think that his wife was cheating on him affirmed that the story of the wife was true. Unfortunately, the man's anger did not decrease.

The wife went upstairs to change while the man was

busy pondering on how to unleash his anger on his wife. When she had changed and came downstairs, she served the dinner. While at the dinner table, the man was not eating but was busy staring at his wife. The wife noticed that the man was staring at her instead of eating; she asked him, 'why are you staring at me?'

The man answered with a question, "Do you know that I can pour this hot soup on you?"

The woman thought he was joking and said, "If you pour it, you will eat the food from my body."

The man who was already engulfed in anger took the plate of food he was eating from and poured it on his wife. Thinking that she will retaliate, he took a knife on the dining table and stabbed the woman. It was at that time their daughter (and their only child) who was below eighteen started shouting and the neighbors were alerted. They rushed into their apartment and saw the woman in the pool of her blood. Some rushed the woman to the hospital while others dragged the man to the police station. Unfortunately, the woman died on her way to the hospital.

While in police custody, the man cried ceaselessly, saying that he did not know what came over him. He said that he loved his wife and had never laid hand on her before. Though the man was given a fair judgment because he was sentenced to five years imprisonment because of their young child but he will surely live in regret that moment of wrath all his life.

Anger has destroyed many families. Eleanor Roosevelt said, *"The word 'Anger' is one word short of 'D-anger."* She's right. Anytime anger is nurtured, there is always a danger ahead

I heard of a man who threw his daughter down from 3 storey building where they lived because he saw her having an affair with her boyfriend in his matrimonial bed. Yes, he had the right to be angry, but you'll agree with me that action was way overboard.

Some people have closed the door they needed for their next level because of anger. Some have killed their loved one because of anger. Some have betrayed the trust of friends and relatives because of anger.

Anger is a monster. It is a demon that we must learn to cast out and resist with all we've got. It is one of the most dangerous tools that Satan uses to wreck lives.

Many people with promising future are languishing in police net as a result of few minutes of uncontrolled anger. A nurtured anger will definitely turn into poison and destroy the vessel carrying it eventually. This is why

God's Word disallows your anger to last a day longer.

> *Be ye angry, and sin not: let not the sun go down upon your wrath -*
> **Ephesians 4:26**

In this Bible study, we are going to explore the root causes of anger, dangers of anger, how to deal appropriately with your anger and or overcome anger moments, and prayers to help us surrender to God's will for our lives, as against surrendering to our anger emotions.

Psychology tells you to "manage anger."

God says, "Deal with anger."

I believe that as we learn and pray in this book, God will touch our heart as we allow Him to mold us into a vessel fit to carry His gospel to the world.

Part 1: Understanding Anger and The Practice of Anger Management

---

"If you get angry easily, it may be because the seed of anger in you has been watered frequently over many years, and unfortunately you have allowed it or even encouraged it to be watered." — Thich Nhat Hanh

---

Chapter 1: Meaning and Types of Anger

"Every day we have plenty of opportunities to get angry, stressed or offended. But what you're doing when you indulge these negative emotions is giving something outside yourself power over your happiness. You can choose to not let little things upset you" - Joel Osteen

Anger is an emotion related to one's inner interpretation of having been offended, wronged, or denied and a tendency to react through retaliation. It is an emotion that involves a strong uncomfortable and emotional response to a perceived provocation.

Anger is an urge to express your feeling of dissatisfaction for something said or done against you.

It is an emotional expression of dissatisfaction; a strong feeling of displeasure, hostility or dislike towards someone or something, usually combined with an urge for vengeance.

There are two types of anger. I like to call them, holy and unholy anger. Good and bad anger. Yes. Not all anger is evil or sinful.

Joyce Meyer said, "Is all anger sin? No, but some of it is. Even God Himself has righteous anger against sin, injustice, rebellion and pettiness. Anger sometimes serves a useful purpose, so it isn't necessarily always a sin."

The right kind of anger is called **_Righteous Indignation_**.

According to Wikipedia, "righteous indignation is typically a reactive emotion of anger over mistreatment, insult, or malice. It is akin to what is called the sense of injustice."

The Bible says:

> *'God is a judge who is perfectly fair, and he is angry with the wicked every day.* Psalm 7:11 (TLB)

God's anger is not towards the persons; else mankind would have become extinct. His anger is towards the wicked works that man exhibits against others daily.

Jesus got angry a couple of times. But His anger was towards injustice and the hardness of heart of the people. The scripture says,

> *And he [Jesus] said to them, "Is it lawful on the Sabbath to do good or to*

do harm, to save life or to kill?" But they were silent. And he looked around at them with anger, grieved at their hardness of heart, and said to the man, "Stretch out your hand." He stretched it out, and his hand was restored.

- Mark 3:4-5

The Passover of the Jews was at hand, and Jesus went up to Jerusalem. In the temple he found those who were selling oxen and sheep and pigeons, and the money-changers sitting there.

And making a whip of cords, he drove them all out of the temple, with the sheep and oxen. And he poured out the coins of the money-changers and overturned their tables.

And he told those who sold the pigeons, "Take these things away; do not make

my Father's house a house of trade." -
John 2:13-16

There are two Greek words used for "anger" in the New Testament. The first is **'thumos,'** which means passion, energy, forthwith boiling up and soon subsiding again. This is the kind of anger that makes us real human (humane). When we see a child abused, or an injustice, we boil against it. We want to fight it. We wish and want something to be done.

This is also the anger that makes us correct a friend when he is in error, or discipline a child when they have missed it.

This type of anger (thumos) is healthy. It is human response to pain, suffering, offence and injustice. It tends to be more seasonal, is usually tied to wrongdoing, and it ends when the situation that created it ends. This is the kind of anger Christ had. That's what Apostle Paul meant when he told believers to "Be angry and sin not." This type of anger is not about you. It's about the rights of others and their welfare or in defense of a principle.

The other Greek word for anger in the New Testament is *"Orge."* This is the strong emotional reaction of displeasure, often leading to plans for revenge or punishment. This is bad anger, the unrighteous anger. It describes what happens when unresolved anger is allowed to bleed into the mind, and build a stronghold there. Wrongs are pondered over and over in the mind, and revenge is planned. This type of anger (orge) is bad and kills. The Bible teaches us to learn to deal with "Orge," unrighteous anger, the anger that 'worketh' not towards the righteousness of God.

Examples of Righteous Anger

"Then the angry king sent the man to the torture chamber until he had paid every last penny due. - Matthew 18:34 (TLB)

In this parable, Jesus talked about a servant who owed the king a lot of money. The Living Bible said he owed approximately 3 million pounds. When the king arrested him and demanded for his money, he fell face down and pleaded for forgiveness. The king had pity on him and forgave him. But on his way home, he met a man owing him about 700 pounds and pounced on him. Despite many pleas from his debtor, he had him arrested and jailed. When the king heard what happened, he got angry and had the servant re-arrested and sent to torture chamber (Matthew 18:23-34 TLB).

Obviously, the king's anger is not because of the amount of money the servant owed him, but the injustice the servant demonstrated on another fellow. That's what the Bible refers to as righteous indignation.

Another example is the case of David and Prophet Nathan (2 Samuel 12). Nathan came to David and told him a story of a very rich man who had many flocks and a poor man who had just a lamb. A guest arrived at the home of the rich man, but instead of killing a lamb from his own flocks for food for the traveler, he took the poor man's lamb and roasted it and served it. Unaware that Nathan was referring to Him, David immediately vowed to find that man and deal with him ruthlessly. 2 Samuel 12:5-6 tells the story...

> *"David was furious. 'I swear by the living God,' he vowed, "any man who*

would do a thing like that should be put to death; he shall repay four lambs to the poor man for the one he stole and for having no pity." (TLB)

Notice that in the above scenarios, the anger was about the injustices, wrongdoings and rights of others being trampled, and not about the persons who got angry. That's the right kind of anger.

On another occasion David fumed:

God, I wish you would kill the wicked! Get away from me, you murderers! They say evil things about you. Your enemies use your name thoughtlessly. Lord, I hate those who hate you; I hate those who rise up against you. I feel only hate for them; They are my enemies (Psalm 139:19–22, NCV).

Here, David called down curses on sworn enemies of

God. He was angry because of ungodly people or activities. As Christ followers, we're totally appropriate getting upset over sin too. Evils such as abuse, racism, pornography, and child sex trafficking should upset us.

If you got annoyed when you saw some kind of maltreatment against others, that's healthy. Even if you couldn't do much, your anger is "thumos," the right kind of anger.

But no matter how disgraceful the people or activities we're condemning, we still aren't justified to sin in our responses. The New Century Version (NCV) of the Bible puts Ephesians 4:26 this way: "When you are angry, do not sin, and be sure to stop being angry before the end of the day."

The Bible also gives us an idea on how best to respond to provocations. Look at the story of Peninnah and

Hannah:

³ Each year Elkanah and his families journeyed to the Tabernacle at Shiloh to worship the Lord of the heavens and to sacrifice to him. (The priests on duty at that time were the two sons of Eli— Hophni and Phinehas.)

⁴ On the day he presented his sacrifice, Elkanah would celebrate the happy occasion by giving presents to Peninnah and her children;

⁵ but although he loved Hannah very much, he could give her only one present, for the Lord had sealed her womb; so she had no children to give presents to.

⁶ Peninnah made matters worse by taunting Hannah because of her barrenness.

⁷ Every year it was the same—Peninnah scoffing and laughing at her as they went to Shiloh, making her cry so much she couldn't eat.

⁸ "What's the matter, Hannah?" Elkanah would exclaim. "Why aren't you eating? Why make such a fuss over having no children? Isn't having me better than having ten sons?"

⁹ One evening after supper, when they were at Shiloh, Hannah went over to the Tabernacle. Eli the priest was sitting at his customary place beside the entrance.

¹⁰ She was in deep anguish and was crying bitterly as she prayed to the Lord.

1 Samuel 1:3-10 (TLB)

Notice the bolded parts of the passage above. Peninnah

was provoking Hannah every time. Hannah had the option of planning revenge. But she directed her anger towards finding a solution to her problem. She went to seek God's face for answers.

William Arthur Ward said, "It is wise to direct your anger towards problems - not people; to focus your energies on answers - not excuses." That's the best way to leverage provocation and anger.

Examples of Unrighteous Anger

*"The older brother was **angry** and wouldn't go in. His father came out and begged him.*

- Luke 15:28 (TLB)

This is the story about the prodigal son. His older brother was angry that he came back and was being celebrated. This is clearly an unrighteous anger, '***Orge.***' It was about his pride, his person, his interests and not about the plight of the younger one who had been missing for a long time. This anger stemmed from pride and envy.

Another interesting example of unrighteous anger is found in Genesis 49:5-7:

> *₅"Simeon and Levi are two of a kind.*
> *They are men of violence and injustice.*
>
> *₆O my soul, stay away from them. May*
> *I never be a party to their wicked*
> *plans. For in their anger they*
> *murdered a man, and maimed oxen*
> *just for fun.*
>
> *₇Cursed be their anger, for it is fierce*
> *and cruel. Therefore, I will scatter their*
> *descendants throughout Israel.*

The actual event that Jacob referenced here happened

in Genesis Chapter 34. Shechem, the son of king Hamor, the Hivite, had raped Dinah, Simeon and Levi's sister. That was immoral. Yes, very wrong. But Simeon and Levi in their anger deceived the entire city and killed all their men and plundered them. No doubt, that was anger taken too far.

Unrighteous anger is unproductive and distorts the purposes of God. As James said, it does not lead to right acts about God's ways (James 1:20).

One obvious sign that anger has turned to sin is when, instead of attacking the problem at hand, we attack the offender, or when the anger is allowed to linger. Another sign of unrighteous anger is when rotten or destructive words begin pour from our lips in response to our dissatisfaction of something. Ephesians 4:15-19 says we are to talk to one another with words that build up and not destroy.

When we also try to exert revenge, then we are in an unrighteous anger because the Bible says that vengeance is of the LORD. Anger also becomes sin when it is allowed to boil over without restraint, resulting in a scenario in which hurt is multiplied, leaving devastation in its wake. Often, the consequences of out-of-control anger are very severe.

Anger also becomes sin when the angry one refuses to be pacified, holds a grudge, or keeps it all inside. This can cause depression and irritability over little things, which are often unrelated to the fundamental problem.

We all need to learn how to deal with the various forms of unrighteous anger. We all need to learn to overcome this devastating emotion of bad anger and allow God's purposes to be made manifest in our lives at all times.

There's a reason anger is classified as part of the works

of the flesh, and put together with the likes of witchcraft, murder and idolatry. And that's because unjust anger is as deadly as murder, witchcraft and idolatry.

> [19] *Now the practices of the sinful nature are clearly evident: they are sexual immorality, impurity, sensuality (total irresponsibility, lack of self-control),* [20] *idolatry, sorcery, hostility, strife, jealousy,* ***fits of anger****, disputes, dissensions, factions [that promote heresies],* [21] *envy, drunkenness, riotous behavior, and other things like these. I warn you beforehand, just as I did previously, that those who practice such things will not inherit the kingdom of God. - Galatians 5:19-21 (AMP)*

If you don't deal with anger, it's capable of preventing you from inheriting the kingdom of God, both here on earth (that is, enjoying the blessings of God) and hereafter. Yes, anger is that serious. It's an instrument of destruction.

Chapter 2: The Spirit of Anger

"To really deal with anger, you need to approach it from a spiritual point of view. You have to bind and cast the spirit of anger out and get healed right deep in your spirit, because that's where the spiritual force of anger is staying and controlling you."

For years, psychologists have tried to describe anger as just a normal emotion that we are all blessed with. They say that when we are angry we are just trying to express a part of us. Hence they recommend various ways to control our actions when we are angry, since we cannot really get over anger completely.

Unfortunately, these psychological exercises, though great, have not helped millions of people fighting anger.

Take the case of Samuel for example. He wrote, *"Please pray for me. I do not understand my anger and I get angry at the slightest of things. When possible, I direct my anger at others, if not I just get very angry at myself. I am trying to devote myself to God and to be obedient to God's commands. I do not want to be angry anymore. I want to learn how to love. I am trying to read the bible every day and spend time with God to learn to be more like him... I am fighting something inside of me that is constantly telling me to sin and go back to drugs... Please pray for me."*

There's no doubt that Samuel is trying to control anger and become better at relating with others. But like he said, his anger is planted deeper in his spirit. He is in a spiritual battle and needs deliverance from this source of anger.

There's nothing wrong with viewing anger as an emotional thing. While that is right, it's only partially right; because the Bible discusses and treats anger as something much more serious, something that is capable of disinheriting someone of his inheritance in Christ.

Galatians 5:19-21 that we quoted earlier in chapter one classifies anger with some deadly works of the flesh. These works of the flesh like murder, witchcraft, idolatry, anger and co. can send anyone to eternal damnation.

Several other scriptures talking about anger didn't try to paint it as something light either. Consider the following:

Scriptures on Anger

Proverbs 22:24-25 (NLT): "Don't befriend angry people or associate with hot tempered people, or you will learn to be like them and endanger your soul.

James 1:20 (NLT): "Human anger does not produce the righteousness God desires."

Psalm 37:8 (NLT): "Stop being angry! Turn from your rage! Do not lose your temper —it only leads to harm."

Proverbs 12:16 (NLT): "A fool is quick-tempered, but a wise person stays calm when insulted."

Proverbs 14:17 (NLT): "Short-tempered people do foolish things, and schemers are hated."

Proverbs 16:32 (KJV): "He that is slow to anger is better than the mighty; and he that ruleth his spirit than he that taketh a city."

Proverbs 29:11 (TLB): "A rebel shouts in anger; a wise man holds his temper in and cools it."

Ecclesiastes 7:9 (KJV): "Be not hasty in thy spirit to be angry: for anger resteth in the bosom of fools."

Ephesians 4:26 – 27 (KJV): "Be ye angry, and sin not: let not the sun go down upon your wrath: Neither give place to the devil."

Matthew 5:21-24 (TLB): "Under the laws of Moses the rule was, 'If you murder, you must die.' But I have added to that rule and tell you that *if you are only angry, even in your own home, you are in danger of judgment!* If you call your friend an idiot, you are in danger of being brought before the court. And if you curse him, you are in danger of the fires of hell.

Colossians 3:8 (AMP): "But now rid yourselves completely of all these things: anger, rage, malice, slander, and obscene (abusive, filthy, vulgar) language from your mouth."

Anger is Spiritual

"Be ye angry, and sin not: let not the sun go down upon your wrath: Neither give place to the devil" - Eph 4:26-27.

The scripture here is saying that our unresolved anger opens the door to our soul (mind, will and emotions) for an evil spirit to come in and oppress us. This evil spirit will encourage and promote anger within the individual, blind the individual from the truth and seek to deceive the individual by exaggerating the irritation and justifying the anger.

So anger is not just an emotional thing. It has a spiritual dimension. Too many people have tried several psychological ways to control their angers and have failed because anger rests deeper in their spirits.

In trying to control your anger, you are controlling your flesh, what you are doing while angry. But that's not controlling the anger. The anger is there, deep down there.

To really deal with anger, you need to approach it from a spiritual point of view. You have to bind and cast the spirit of anger out and get healed right deep in your spirit, because that's where the spiritual force of anger is staying and controlling you.

Eunice Kihara needed healing from anger. She wrote: "I have been so angry for 7 years because the person who I thought was the love of my life was a cheater, a liar and abandoned me when I needed him the most. I got pregnant. This has seriously affected my life. There are times I feel like committing suicide. I am still so angry at him and at life that it's actually affecting my new relationship. Pray for me to get guidance from God on what to do and for him to take away this pain and anger and resentment."

The spirit of anger can enter a person through pain and disappointment of the past. If the victim fails to identify the right source of his anger and continues to try many psychological ways to control and manage anger, he will continue to fail. He will continue to wonder why he is trying to control himself but don't know why he keeps lashing out the way he does.

The spirit of anger may also enter a person through unforgiveness (Matthew 18:21-35), through any kind of occult involvement, or through sexual relations with another person who has such evil spirits.

Other ways that the spirit of anger can also enter and begin to control a person include: family line anger transfer, abuse, failed parenting, divorce of parents, envy, etc. As we discover the sources and causes of anger and begin to address them in prayer, we can expect complete healing and deliverance from the demonic stronghold of anger.

Chapter 3: Causes (and Sources) of Anger

"19 My dear brothers and sisters, take note of this: Everyone should be quick to listen, slow to speak and slow to become angry, 20 because human anger does not produce the righteousness that God desires." - James 1:19-20 (NIV)

Anger does not produce the righteousness of God. The scripture says it should be the last thing we ever become. Let's look at some of the sources of anger.

1. Pain or Maltreatment From the Past

Janine wants to be free from anger. She wrote, "I have a

problem with my anger. I shout and I say bad things when I am angry. I know it's because deep down I am just hurt, but because I try to be strong it's like the hurt converts in to anger. But I feel so awful after. I'm ruining my life and others. I hope I can become a better person for myself and others."

It's good that Janine realized her anger came from her past hurt. This mixture of pain and guilt is cumulative and it bursts in anger when new offenses remind us of past experiences.

Most of us presume that hurtful events in the past will be forgotten and will have no effect on the future. That is not true. Past hurts do not just go away, nor does guilt simply disappear after a wrong response to a situation. Unless these experiences are resolved through repentance and forgiveness, we will continue to experience bouts of anger when our tension points are triggered.

One mother wrote, "Please pray for my daughter Hillary. She has anger issues and it is definitely from her childhood. My parents favored all the grandkids over her even still to this day; told her it was because of something that happened at the hospital the night she was born so that is why she is treated differently. She is now 25 years old. It has really taken a toll on her emotionally and mentally and has caused havoc in her life. She was also raped at 14 and date raped at 23 so that on top of this plus having a father that has had nothing much to do with her, with all of this it has just caused her to be very angry and constant fight with depression. Please pray, thank you!"

In order to effectively deal with anger, one would need to first and foremost try to recognize pain from the past. The following situations often lead us into bitterness, where we typically lash out in wrath, revenge, or other hurtful responses.

- The pain of rejection, especially in childhood.

- The reaction to unchangeable features of our lives. One who experiences ridicule due to physical body features that's not of his making will be exceptionally sensitive to anyone else who ridicules him or others. The anger he feels is motivated by a desire for just vengeance of anyone who mocks others.

- The pain of favoritism

- The pain of false accusations

The combination of guilt and hurt that surrounds the

memory of these experiences activates anger when we hear of or face similar situations.

2. Generational Stronghold

Jay requested for prayers for help with anger. But he was able to recognize that this anger did not start with him. He says, "Please pray for me that the chains of anger will be taken away by God from my family. I have this anger that comes like a volcano, probably as a result of my Dad who is also an angry man. I tend to shout at my kids and I am seeing this anger now with my seven year old son and 5 year old daughter. Lord God please help me."

It's obvious that the chain of anger is being passed on from past generation in Jay's family. I will not be surprised if further probing reveals anger problems in his past 4th and 5th generations.

The Bible is clear that mannerisms, attitudes and behaviors can be learned and passed on to generations. Genesis 49:5-7 gives a very clear and powerful picture of this fact.

> *Simeon and Levi are brethren; instruments of cruelty are in their habitations.*
>
> *O my soul, come not thou into their secret; unto their assembly, mine honour, be not thou united: for in their anger they slew a man, and in their selfwill they digged down a wall.*
>
> *Cursed be their anger, for it was fierce; and their wrath, for it was cruel: I will divide them in Jacob, and scatter them in Israel. -*

In this scripture, Simeon and Levi were cursed because of what they did in anger. As we've noted in chapter one, this thing they did is found in Genesis chapter 34. They wiped out an entire city in anger and revenge of their sister's abuse. This anger became a major weakness, which passed on to their generations. Moses came from the Levi family line. He was a very hot tempered man. Despite his many encounters with God, his anger prevented him from entering the Promised Land.

> *And there went a man of the house of Levi, and took to wife a daughter of Levi. And the woman conceived, and bare a son: and when she saw him that he was a goodly child, she hid him three months -* **Exodus 2:1-2**

> *And it came to pass, as soon as he came nigh unto the camp, that he saw the calf, and the dancing: and Moses' anger waxed hot, and he cast the tables out of his hands, and brake them beneath the mount -* **Exodus 32:19**

People with a history of anger in their family will have severe anger issues unless they go through a process of spiritual deliverance. That is the only way to deal with such angers.

There are some angers that you can easily determine that it is not natural. People with such anger never get appeased until they have done things that are terrible and stupid, things that they end up regretting later. That kind of anger is not normal. They are being fueled by evil spirits from one's family lineage. However, there is deliverance in Jesus Christ to the one who asks in faith.

3. Wrong Modeling

It's been said that the best way children learn and copy habits is by observation. If parents often lash out in anger and use anger as a means to get their needs met, children in that home will unconsciously copy anger. And that will become a source of anger in their lives even when they are grownups. It's no wonder the Bible says,

> *Train up a child in the way he should go: and when he is old, he will not depart from it. -* Proverbs 22:6 (KJV)

Parents must prayerfully learn to help their kids copy behaviors that glorify God in their lives as they grow up. Someone has said that "Children are great imitators. So give them something great to imitate."

To fully deal with anger we must come with open hearts and ask ourselves serious questions to help us identify the sources of anger in our lives. When we truly identify the sources of our anger, we are halfway through with finding freedom.

4. Frustration of Goals

If you're dealing with a lot of problems in your life right now, you might find yourself getting angry more easily than usual, or getting angry at unrelated things. People who seem not to accomplish their goals can have the feeling of anger develop in them. When a person cannot cater for his responsibility because of lack of fund, he will be unhappy. The anger some people have vented on others come as a result of frustration from their seeming failures.

5. Offence

Amnon was the first son of David. He lusted after his half-sister, Tamar, who was Absalom's sister. He wanted to have Tamar at all cost and through the counsel of his friend Jonadab, he got her. He forcefully slept with her and after that he hated her and drove her out disgracefully. This infuriated Absalom and he sought a way to vent his anger on his brother. Opportunity provided itself and he killed Amnon.

When people say or do something rude which upsets or embarrasses others, or violates their rights, it becomes an offence. This can be a major source of anger.

The scripture counsel us on how to relate with others. It advices us to be courteous and polite in order to minimize offences. That's because *"even if you can tell what you'll do when you're angry, you'll not be able to tell what another person will do in anger."*

People have been poured acid, while some others have been stabbed because of offence. You can only minimize "offence" coming from you by obeying God's Words to be courteous and polite in relating with others.

On the other hand, the Bible has given us a clue on how to handle ourselves when offended. First, Jesus said,

"...Offenses will certainly come, but woe to the one they come through!"- (Luke 17:1 - Holman Christian Standard Bible). That is to say that the one that causes offence willfully and makes others stumble will face severe divine consequences. However, it is not our responsibility to execute the judgment. And that's what we do when we become angry, or allow anger to cause us to sin when offended. Romans 12:19 says:

"My friends, do not try to punish others when they wrong you, but wait for God to punish them with his anger. It is written: 'I will punish those who do wrong; I will repay them,' says the Lord" (NCV).

7. Expectations

When people make promises and fail to keep them, we tend to hold that against them and become angry at their failure to fulfill our expectations. When we expect certain conducts or benefits from others—especially those who are closest to us—and they do not act as we expect, this can also lead to anger.

8. Pride

When someone's perception or point of views are not respected or valued, it can trigger anger. This is why it is easy to find anger in a place of serious argument.

Pride makes us assume authority that does not belong to us. We find ourselves step into another's jurisdiction with efforts to exert control. In turn we find our points and opinions rejected, leading to conflict and bouts of rage and bitterness.

Apart from others' rejection of our opinions and points of view, our individual perception of how things should be and done can also be the reason for anger. It's very important to understudy people you relate with and endeavor to respect their opinions, even when you're not going to need it.

9. Misunderstanding About God

Most times we don't see the big picture. We may take one look at the situation and declare that God is unfair. This view often produces anger.

For example, Job cursed the day that he was born because he viewed God as unfair (Job 3:1-3). David became very upset when he saw the wicked prosper. He said, "When I thought to know this, it was too painful for me" (Psalm 73:16). Jonah became very angry because he thought that God was biased. "But it displeased Jonah exceedingly, and he was very angry" (Jonah 4:1).

A woman who has done her best to serve God when she was single may be angry when she sees others she witnessed their marriage dedicating their babies while she is still expecting to have one. She is not angry with the woman dedicating the baby but she is just angry that what happens for others has refused to happen for her.

Some people have had mix feelings for others that are succeeding in life. They may be happy that they are doing well but on the other hand sad that they themselves are still struggling.

If one seems to be struggling in life while his mates are doing fine, it can trigger anger which may also degenerate to hate and jealousy. This is simply a misunderstanding about God.

10. Loss

Life is full of ups and downs. Sometimes we'll encounter losses as result of our bad decisions or just what life throws at us. When situations like that occur and are not handled with proper prayers and counseling, we might become frustrated, hate ourselves, and unknowingly develop anger deep inside of us.

Yayandrei wrote, "Please pray for me. I hate myself for making wrong decisions. Sometimes I hate the people who treated me unfairly. I want to release all my worries."

People have lost money or house to fire accident or financial institution. People have lost beloved ones, business opportunities, lucrative jobs and other valuables. The anger at self and frustration that come as a result of these losses can sometimes lead to anger resting deep inside of us and even lead to mental depression.

11. Normal Emotion

As we've earlier noted, some anger issues are not that bad. They may just be a way we express our displeasure of something. Provided this anger does not continue till the next day or result in revenge, and or the use of cursing and hurtful words, and it's not too frequent, we may not need to worry so much about it.

But the problem is that most anger issues are strong enough to produce really bad consequences. The Bible says it's possible for us to get angry. But that we should not sin in our anger (Ephesians 4:26). If your anger is not leading to sin, then you're safe.

There may be other things that can cause one to be angry not listed here. If you can pin point what usually makes you angry, you're half way delivered from it. The point is to learn to deal with anger appropriately by looking beyond your anger and trying to determine the real source or sources of your anger.

Chapter 4: The Dangers of Anger

"If you are patient in one moment of anger, you will escape a hundred days of sorrow" - Chinese Proverb

A wise man said that "Anger is an acid that can do more harm to the vessel in which it is stored than to anything on which it is poured." Anger can destroy many beautiful destinies.

1. Anger will cost you your internal peace

Anger is a spiritual robber and a destroyer of joy and peace. This is why people who are in rage cannot think straight. No one enjoys internal peace when angry.

2. Anger can create stress

Experts say that our blood pressure usually goes high in a state of anger. Maya Angelou said, "Bitterness is like cancer. It eats upon the host. But anger is like fire. It burns it all clean." Anger can create stress which is disastrous to health.

3. Anger can lead to bitterness and unforgiveness

A pastor friend who had heart condition said that all the attempts by medical personnel to recover his health failed woefully until he forgave his father whom he was angry with. Until he decided to release his father in his heart his health deteriorated.

Many people are busy consuming drugs which has no effect on their sickness because the root of that sickness is buried in their anger which has led to bitterness and unforgiveness. That is why it is said that "Anger is often more hurtful than the injury that caused it."

4. Anger is an ally to the long arm of the law.

Anytime anger is being nurtured, the long arm of the law is being alerted. Many people have been arrested, charged and sentenced severely because of actions they took in anger. Some are awaiting trial for years now because of anger.

A pastor friend of mine who went to 'Kirikiri' for prison evangelism told me a story of an encounter he had in one of his prison visitations. As he was ministering the word of God to the inmates who were awaiting trial, he observed that one of them was crying profusely. My friend said he knew within him that he was not crying as a result of conviction of the message he was preaching.

So when he finished his message, he approached him

and demanded to know why he was crying when he was ministering. The middle aged man told him that he was not a bad person. He said that he was a bricklayer working for one of his customers that hired him to do something for him. Then came a young man from nowhere and began to drag his shovel with him. He said that this guy claimed that the shovel belongs to him. In the midst of the hot argument a fight erupted. He took a stick and hit the young man and he died instantly. That was how he found himself in prison. He said that he has been there for a very long time and his case has not been tried.

Of a truth, "if you are patient in one moment of anger, you will escape a hundred days of sorrow." May the LORD give us wisdom and grace to learn how to respond to those who provoke and make us angry.

5. Anger discomforts others

Anger is contagious and it spreads like a wild fire. It is difficult to be happy in a company of angry people. In a home when one member of the family is angry, others will be uncomfortable. If the man is not happy, the comfort of the rest members of the family is at stake. You cannot be comfortable around someone that is angry. Anger is transferable and it can create discomfort.

6. Anger can make you do things you'll regret all your life

A man had a usual misunderstanding with his wife and went to bed. Out of anger, the woman went and boiled hot water and poured on the man. The shout of the man alerted neighbors. Unfortunately, he died on his way to the hospital.

No doubt, this woman will live to remember this all her

life. Except God's healing, she'll be hunted by this action orchestrated by one moment of rage.

7. Anger affects your health

The constant flood of stress chemicals and associated metabolic changes that go with recurrent unresolved anger can eventually cause harm to many different systems of the body. Some of the short and long-term health problems that have been linked to anger include:

- headache

- digestion problems, such as abdominal pain

- sleeplessness

- enlarged anxiety

- sadness, despair, depression

- high blood pressure

- skin problems, such as eczema

- heart attack

- Anger ups your stroke risk

Anger is not your friend. As Charles Spurgeon said, "Do not say, 'I cannot help having a bad temper.' Friend, you must help it. Pray to God to help you overcome it at once, for either you must kill it, or it will kill you. You cannot carry a bad temper into heaven."

Chapter 5: How to Deal With Anger

"But now rid yourselves [completely] of all these things: anger, rage, malice, slander, and obscene (abusive, filthy, vulgar) language from your mouth." - Colossians 3:8 (AMP)

The Bible says we should get rid of anger, rage, malice, slander and vulgar language. God didn't say we should find ways to manage our bad anger, pamper it or get used to it. God will certainly not ask us to do what we cannot do. And more importantly, it is to our advantage that we deal with these loopholes because they are capable of hindering us from fulfilling God's plans for our lives.

You can overcome your anger issues today if you desire. What you need is to stop shifting blames, take responsibility and ask God for help. Yes, you can overcome anger. God will give you the strength to do so if you desire. As you do, God's power is made available for your complete victory, already obtained at the Cross.

If you're ready to deal with anger, here are steps you can take to get started…

1. Review your conviction about anger

As we've noted in this book, anger is a serious issue. It can destroy a person's life and destroy the lives of others. It's not something minor that we can handle by just will power and learning some new psychological maneuvers. It's a deadly weapon of the devil, whose ultimate aim is to steal, kill and destroy, here on earth, and finally prevents one from entering the kingdom of God.

Learn to see anger as the Bible sees it. Don't trivialize it. Acknowledge that anger is a powerful enemy that you must deal with carefully so it won't hurt you and others around you.

2. Admit the anger you in you

The Bible says that those who cover their faults will not prosper. But if we confess and forsake them, we'll obtain mercy and find healing (Proverbs 28:13, 1 John 1:9).

Don't try to deny or subdue your anger. Tell yourself the truth and be honest with God. If we do not admit our guilt, we do not find help.

3. Identify the sources of your anger problem

It has been said, "The issue is never the issue." The Scripture refers to anger as a fruit, which means that it must be coming from a tree. Most anger problems stem from something deeper. Ask God to help you figure out what's causing you to feel angry, so you can address the issue from the root. Also consider these common sources of anger:

- Pain or maltreatment from the past

- Generational stronghold

- Wrong modeling

- Frustration of goals

- Offence

- Unmet expectations from others

- Pride

- Loss

- Misunderstanding about God's ways (unanswered prayers)

- Insecurity (inferiority complex)

- etc

Identifying the sources of your anger will help your deliverance faster.

4. Wait on the LORD in prayer

When we pray, we give room to the Holy Spirit to uproot the seeds of evil in our deepest parts. We give room to God to heal and deliver us from whatever stronghold is holding us bound.

I strongly recommend that you take your anger

problems to God in prayers and fasting. Jesus said there are spiritual cases that can only be resolved by prayer and fasting (Matthew 17:21). I believe that anger problems are one of those cases.

When we seek deliverance from a habit or stronghold in fasting and prayer, we allow God's light to shine in our deepest parts. Isaiah 58:6 says,

> *"[Rather] is this not the fast which I choose, To undo the bonds of wickedness, To tear to pieces the ropes of the yoke, To let the oppressed go free And break apart every [enslaving] yoke?" (AMP)*

When we fast and pray to seek deliverance and break the yoke of Satan on our lives and that of others, we are in God's will. And when we do God's will, we receive His blessings and victory.

This book comes with powerful prayer points and guidelines for dealing with anger. As you seek God with these prayers, you'll be delivered of anger issues and any other stronghold that is holding you bound.

5. Prayerfully forgive

Pray and ask God to help you forgive anyone you're holding any anger against who may have hurt you. Colossians 3:13 says, "Be gentle and ready to forgive; never hold grudges. Remember, the Lord forgave you, so you must forgive others" (TLB).

If you're holding onto anger against someone who has hurt you, you can't be in a right relationship with God. Don't wait until you feel like forgiving because you probably never will. Instead, decide to forgive despite your feelings, and as you trust God to help you with the forgiveness process, your feelings will change along the way.

6. Prayerfully re-channel your energy

Instead of exercising your energy in pain, anger and vengeance, ask God to help you redirect your energy to positive actions that are useful and productive. God will show you little things you could start doing that will not just empower you, but also empower others around you.

7. Plan how to respond to subsequent provocations

So long as we are still in the world, offenses and provocations will continue to come. However, we are not to be ruled by these negative emotions. We who are in obedience to God must overcome these attacks with God's love from time to time. So rehearse in your mind what you can say and do to respond wisely to difficult people or tense situations you may encounter that can prompt anger in you. Then, when you're faced with them, you'll have a plan to follow.

8. Surrender to God

Are you angry that your prayers have not been answered? Or are you angry at some of the bad things that you had to go through in life?

Well, you're not alone. Many of us have been angry at God at one time or the other. The only way to deal with this is to be honest with God and talk to Him about it. When we honestly and humbly go to Him and say, "Heavenly Father, I'm not happy that You allowed these things to happen to me," we'll find His love overshadow us, and His Spirit teaching us things we didn't know before.

In his book, *Surviving in an Angry World: Finding Your Way to Personal Peace*, bestselling author and pastor, Charles F. Stanley, counsels, "If you're angry at God because of something that He allowed to happen to you, be honest with Him about your anger but then let go of it quickly after you express it."

If we do not address our anger against God quickly, the devil will further poison our soul with deeper evils. We must be willing to place our trust in God - no matter what - since He loves us completely, knows what's best for the life He has given us and only allows what can help us grow into a stronger person to come our way.

9. Decide that you'll never go to bed angry

God's Word tells us, "Do not let the sun go down while you are still angry, and do not give the devil a foothold" (Eph. 4:27). When we go to bed angry, we're in disobedience to God. So it can make us not to sleep well, get attacked spiritually and expose our body to sickness.

Resolve that you'll never put yourself in such misery. As much as possible, take steps to resolve any anger moment that showed up within the day. Then commit others that you couldn't handle to God in prayers and ask Him to cleanse your mind and spirit.

10. Discuss your anger with family members and loved ones

Most times misunderstandings occur as a result of lack of proper communication. It's also possible that anger has created a huge gap between you and your family members or friends. So take steps to talk with your family members and close friends about specific ways that you can strengthen your relationships with each of them.

If you feel anger has affected your relationships in any way, apologize to each other, pray together, identify positive steps each person can take to rebuild the relationship, and move on with those steps.

11. Learn to resolve misunderstandings wisely

The truth is even with all the steps you take to deal with anger, you'll still encounter plenty of conflicts, misunderstandings and skirmishes that you must deal with wisely to create positive results from them. When dealing with conflicts, refuse to respond in anger to what other people say or do. Instead, listen quietly until they're done expressing themselves. Then identify your part in the conflict and ask God to help you say what you need to say with kindness and respect.

Learn from conflict and make whatever changes God leads you to make from what you've learned.

12. Learn to sometimes accept defeat in an argument for peace to reign

I once had an argument with an elderly man who worked for us as a gateman. He left his duty post without permission and never came back until late in the night. He went to a party and drank himself to stupor. As I confronted him to ask why he left the gate open until the mid-night, he began to say all manner of rubbish things against me and even threatened to stab me.

"What!"

I was angry enough to hit him that night, but I prayed for peace in my heart, held myself and walked away. It was later I realized why he was vibrating and threatening to kill me that night.

He had accepted to work as a security man in his old age

because he had no other option. He also did not have a male child (talk about tradition), and was getting to 70 years. He was bitter about life and what it had done to him. Most times when he saw my children playing in the compound, he would be filled with hatred, jealousy and anger.

Now, imagine if I had tried to talk back at this man that night. Imagine if I had insisted on standing on my right and let him know I'm the boss. Most likely the end result would have been very bad that night.

The man later apologized when he came back to his senses. That was how I got to know what he was battling with all inside himself.

By walking away that night, I actually won. By walking away, I defeated the devil and won the right to minister God's love to him.

By the way, it was not his fault that he does not have a male child, and maybe it's also not his fault he needed to work at that age of his life to make ends meet. But it's also not my fault.

By learning to walk away from arguments where we need to prove how right we are, we can actually save the day, win the real battle and win the right to minister God's love to others. Remember, if you accept defeat in an argument, it does not make you a loser; it only means you are wiser.

13. Learn to control yourself while responding to people when they are angry

Learning how not to respond to others in anger when they are angry, either at you, or at others, is a great way to maintain your edge over the spirit of anger. The Bible offers us a few suggestions on how to reply to angry people.

- Speak gently and slowly (Proverbs 15:1)

- Do not join the person to be angry (Ecclesiastes 7:9)

- If possible, only listen and don't respond immediately (James 1:19)

- If you must speak, look beyond the angry words; ask sincere questions, like, "why do you feel that way? Please help me to understand what you are saying."

- Have a servant attitude. Think of the wellbeing of the person angry. Don't put yourself first. Ask

"What can I do to help solve the problem?" (Philippians 2:3-5)

- Forgive in advance. Pray for a heart to forgive offences even before they come (Colossians 3:13)

- Rebuke the spirit of anger. If somebody is fuming and lashing out in rage, silently rebuke the spirit of anger. Whatever you bind on earth will be bound in heaven (Matthew 16:18-19 & Matthew 18:18-19)

- Compliment the angry person. ("You are the best husband in the whole world.")

- Accept and confess personal wrongs done the person and ask for their forgiveness. "I am sorry" is just a three-letter sentence but it can heal wounds that thousands of dollars cannot.

- Prayerfully surrender any personal rights and expectations that the person has disrespected unto the Lord. Something like, "Lord Jesus, I yield to you my right for others to appreciate me. Empower me by Your Spirit in this situation to help this person"

- Pray and ask the Lord to open the door of opportunity for you to minister His Love and do something good for the individual that is angry. Pray that the Lord will heal and set him free from anger.

- Ask God to fill your heart with His grace of LOVE that you may show God's love to the individual unconditionally.

14. Take a time out

The exercise to count to ten when angry is not just for kids, it also works for adults. Before reacting to a tensed situation, take a few moments to breathe deeply and count to ten. Slowing down can help to diffuse your temper. Sometimes walking out of the scene of provocation like the way I did can help in reducing the weight of the anger on you.

15. Get some exercise

Physical exercise can provide an outlet for your emotions especially if you are about to erupt. If you feel your anger is about to go out of control, go for a brisk walk, or run, or spend some time doing other favorite physical activities. Physical activity stimulates various brain chemicals that can leave you feeling happier and more relaxed than you were before you walked out.

16. Get some spiritual help and counseling

If you're really struggling with anger issues, talking to a spiritually mature person can help you a lot. You need someone to listen to you and agree with you in prayers.

There's a word of caution here. Psychological exercises, though great, cannot really deal with anger, because anger is spiritual. You need a release of God's power into your spirit to uproot the seed of anger.

17. Try to keep yourself busy with things (within reason) that turn you on.

God's word says that a merry heart does good like a

medicine (Proverbs 17:22). Joy is not only a cure to depression, it can also diffuse anger. You cannot be joyful and angry at the same time. Do everything within your power to keep peace of mind within your life and home.

However you must ensure that things that turn you on are not health/life threatening. Some people smoke, drink alcohol or visit brothel to have sex with harlots as a cure to their anger. They are solving one problem but at the same time creating many more. Obviously, that's not what I am asking you to do.

I have no doubt that the above 17 tips will help you deal with and overcome anger issues. More importantly however, I have learned that the best and fastest way to obtain victory over any inner battle, obtain deliverance from spiritual strongholds and overcome demonic entrapments, is to ask the Holy Spirit how to handle the issue. Most times, the Holy Spirit could reveal a simple action or step to take, quite different from what you have read, or He may inspire you on one of the steps you have read. Once God has given this revelation through the Holy Spirit, simply muster the courage to obey. Inside that obedience is your freedom.

Part 2: Prayers to Deal With Anger

"People won't have time for you if you are always angry or complaining."

- Stephen Hawking

Chapter 6: Dealing With Anger Through Prayers

"Fervent prayers produce phenomenal results." - Woodrow Kroll

Anger is a serious issue that we all must deal with. It opens door for other evil spirits to come in, live and torment one's soul. However, prayer is God's gift and opportunity we can all use to open our hearts to God for help and deliverance from whatever affliction we are going through. We have assurance that when we pray, that we will receive answers to our prayers, especially as we pray according to God's will. 1 John 5:14 says,

"This is the confidence we have in approaching

God: that if we ask anything according to his will, he hears us."

Be rest assured that desiring and praying for healing and deliverance from anger is God's will. God wants us to deal with any kind of negative emotion that is capable of stealing our joy, hurting others and preventing us from entering His kingdom.

How to Use These Prayers

1. **Pray with fasting:** Anger is deeper than the surface reasons for getting angry. The root causes need to be dealt with and the spirit cast out. Fasting will prepare your mind and spirit to be receptive to the Holy Spirit's direction while praying. You may fast in any way that you are comfortable with. There's no mandated fast that you must do. What matters is that you come

before God in humility and be ready for a move of God in your heart.

2. **Pray for Many Days:** There are over 100 prayer points below, targeted towards complete deliverance from anger (and it's friends – hate, jealousy, bitterness, stress, pain, etc), all arranged under different headings. I recommend that you pick one or two headings and pray the prayer points per day. Assuming you decide to pray Prayer 1 and Prayer 2 for today, and continue with Prayer 3 and Prayer 4 tomorrow. It means that you'll complete the prayer points in about 5 days. But if you decide to pray the prayers one day at a time, it means you'll likely complete the prayers in 10 days. The idea is for you not to be in haste to recite the prayers and say you're done. You need

to be soaked in the prayers and have an encounter with God.

3. **Believe in your prayers:** God will answer your prayers. All you need to do is believe and pray. Most times, you may not witness some sky shakings and fallings, or any special physical signs and manifestations. A few times you may witness some physical vibrations, signs or manifestations. Whatever the case, understand that we must not judge ourselves and prayers based on physical experiences, but by what God has said in the scriptures. And He has said that as you pray, your prayers will be answered.

4. **Yield to the Holy Spirit while praying:** Don't forget that the prayers below are to be guidelines. While you pray, the Holy Spirit will guide your

thoughts. He will add more or subtract from the prayer words. You may feel like praying some other things or for other areas not stated. Don't be overly static. Be flexible and pray as you are led by the Holy Spirit. He is there with you to guide and help you obtain complete victory.

5. **Recommended prayer times:** While you may pray at any time, it is highly recommended that you select any of the time sessions below.

- 12:00am – 1:00am (Midnight Session)

- 3:00Am – 4:00Am (Early Morning Session)

- 6:00am – 7:00am (Morning Session)

- 12:00 – 1:00pm (Midday Session)

- 3:00pm – 4:00pm (Afternoon Session)

- 9:00pm – 10:00pm (Night Session)

You may choose any of the sessions and pray for your chosen number of days. There are no mandates, which means you could chose afternoon session today and pray, and chose midnight session tomorrow and pray. Whatever is convenient for your schedule is welcome.

Prayer 1: A Prayer of Confession and Total Surrender

The first thing we want to do when we come before God is to humble ourselves, confess any known sins to the LORD and ask the Holy Spirit to search our hearts, bring to our knowledge hidden sins that might be there keeping us away from the goodness of God.

So dedicate today to humble yourself before God and let the Holy Spirit into your life. The scripture says in **2 Chronicles 7:14,** *"If my people, who are called by my name, will humble themselves and pray and seek my face and turn from their wicked ways, then I will hear from heaven, and I will forgive their sin and will heal their land."*

Direction

Begin each of your prayer sessions with praises and thanksgiving to God. Sing and Worship God. This sets the atmosphere right for supernatural manifestation.

Scripture for Reflection

Psalm 51

Prayers

1. *"Heavenly Father,*

I come before You in humility this day and surrender to Your Authority and Power.

I plead that You have mercy upon me O LORD. Forgive me in every way I have sinned against THEE. Forgive my anger, hatred, unforgivensss, jealousy, malice and pride.

Forgive all my false perceptions about life.

LORD, please bring to my notice every sin resting deep in my heart that I am pampering, tolerating and feeding. As I confess them today O LORD, may your mercy and the blood of Jesus Christ begin to speak for me in them.

In Jesus Name.

---

2. Heavenly Father,

I believe and confess that Jesus Christ is Your only begotten son through whom we obtain salvation. And I hereby declare the LORDSHIP of Jesus Christ over my life, over my spirit, soul and body.

LORD Jesus, please come into my life and take Your place henceforth as the LORD and Savior. Let Your Blood cleanse me of all sins resting in my thoughts, feelings, actions and perceptions.

In Jesus name.

---

3. O LORD,

Please create in me a new heart, a heart that will always seek after THEE. A Heart that forgives and thinks of the wellbeing of others first.

Let Your Spirit take over my life and direct me from today forward.

Lead me on the path of righteousness and cause me to live a holy and sanctified life.

In Jesus name.

---

4. From today, LORD JESUS,

I declare that I am separated from sin. I declare that I

have victory over anger, unforgiveness and all sins resting in my feelings and emotions.

I declare that You, Jesus Christ is my LORD and my Savior. I declare that I am a new creature, and old things, old habits, old ways of doing and seeing things have now passed away.

I declare that I will grow daily in the knowledge of God henceforth.

In Jesus Name.

Read the Following Scriptures

- John 14:15-18,

- John 15:26,

- John 16:13-14

- Romans: 8:11-16

Sing (Songs of the Holy Spirit)

- Sing as many songs that come into your heart

- https://www.youtube.com/watch?v=XPPMSfCdUng

- https://www.youtube.com/watch?v=UqU_32v0RI

- https://www.youtube.com/watch?v=aH0p8tXMXlc

Invite the Holy Spirit into Your Life

5. *Dear Holy Spirit,*

I welcome you into my life. I surrender my spirit, soul and body unto You this moment. Let your presence be revealed in my life, in the mighty name of Jesus Christ.

6. *Holy Spirit,*

Open my spiritual ears to hear and follow You leading from today. Empower me to walk in the path ordained to establish my destiny. From this day forward, may I never depart from Thy presence. Be my guide as I navigate this earth

In Jesus Name.

7. Holy Spirit,

I dedicate this entire prayer season unto Thee. Lead me to pray the right way and cause me to obtain victory over all the evil deposits of anger in my life, in Jesus name.

Bind the Spirits of Distraction | Plead the Blood

8. O LORD,

Today and every other day in this season of waiting on the LORD, I bind every spirit of distraction and weakness.

I bind every spirit of forgetfulness and spiritual laxity.

I cast these evil spirits into abyss in Jesus name.

9. I forbid distraction and weakness of the body this movement and all through the coming days of my waiting on the LORD.

I declare that I have strength and power to wait on the Lord, In Jesus name.

---

10. My LORD and my God, I immerse my spirit, soul and body completely in the blood of Jesus Christ.

Blood of Jesus Christ! Blood of Jesus Christ! Blood of Jesus Christ! Blood of Jesus Christ! Blood of Jesus Christ! Blood of Jesus Christ! Blood of Jesus Christ!

Deliver and protect me and my family henceforth, in Jesus name.

---

11. For according to the book of Exodus 12:13 'the blood

shall be to me for a token upon my life and family, and when the angel of death shall see the blood, he shall pass over and the plague shall not rest upon me and my house hold.'

According to the book of Revelation 12:11, **I overcome the enemy by the Blood of Jesus Christ.**

Therefore, I call upon the everlasting Blood of Jesus Christ right now to erect a wall of protection over my life and family in Jesus name.

---

12. According to Zechariah 9:11, **"by the blood of thy covenant I have sent forth thy prisoners out of the pit where is no water"**

For this, O LORD, I decree today that I have my freedom, deliverance, and breakthrough.

By the Blood of Jesus Christ and His covenant, I come

out of every pit where I have hitherto been buried. And I claim my total healing and deliverance from anger, pain, sickness and weakness

Thank You Jesus, for my victory, In Jesus name I pray. Amen

Prayer 2: Power to Exercise Forgiveness Now and Every Day

"And be ye kind one to another, tenderhearted, forgiving one another, even as God for Christ's sake hath forgiven you."

- Ephesians 4:32.

The following discussion on forgiveness is culled from the book, Inner Peace, by Daniel C. Okpara.

"Forgiveness is not easy, especially when we have been hurt, betrayed and treated unfairly by the people involved. Take the case of Pamela for example. How would she go about forgiving someone who is cheating on her and is not willing to repent?

"However, the reason God asks us to forgive is more for ourselves, than for the people who have hurt us. When we forgive others, we directly release ourselves from the judgment of the offenders and find strength to access what God has in store for us.

"Who do you forgive?

1. Forgive Yourself

"Sometimes we blame ourselves unfairly and build up regrets over what we did and didn't do well to contribute to the situation we are faced with at the moment. And no doubt, one may have missed it and even messed up so many times in the past and missed so many opportunities. But to move forward, you have to let go. You have to forgive yourself.

2. Forgive God

"Sometimes we also get in the web of thinking that

maybe God did not care enough. "Maybe if God had kept this from happening, I would be fine," we seem to always think. But blaming God never helps anyone out of his predicaments. Rather, it gets things worse.

"It sounds odd to say this but just in case you feel God did not care enough, forgive God and move on. Actually, God never contributed to make our situations worse. He actually loves us more than we think.

3. Forgive the Government

"We might also be caught up in the ring of thinking maybe if we had had the right policy or infrastructure from the government, this situation might not be like this. We might be right in our thoughts, but to move forward, we must trace all sources of blames and get rid of them.

"Forgive your government, clear yourself of any form of

bitterness towards the leaders and release yourself to your blessings.

"You could say something like, '*Well, I know that my government and the people that lead us haven't done so well. But I forgive them henceforth. And I receive grace to quit blaming people in government and move on doing the best I can*'

4. Forgive Your Parents Or Children.

"Most times in my life I have blamed my parents for not doing their best to put my siblings and me on equal standing with others in life. And apart from that, my childhood memory is filled with unusual wickedness meted out to my parents and us by the extended family members. I was always keeping these records praying to pay back at the appropriate time.

"But I found out I've got to let these things go if I'll have to move on with my life. Whatever wrongs your parents or family members, whether paternal or maternal family members, have done to you in the past, forgive and receive God's peace and move on. Clear those records off your mind.

5. Forgive Those Who Have Hurt You

"Forgive those who betrayed you. Forgive those who made you lose the contract or job and never cared. Forgive the cheating partner. Forgive the hurts. Forgive those who took you for granted. Forgive those willfully owing you and not wanting to pay back.

"Forgive. Forgive. Forgive.

"Forgive and receive God's peace in your life and an unusual open door. Withdraw all plans and setups to avenge in any matter.

6. Make Amends Where Necessary

"Find out within yourself if you've done things that hurt someone in the past and take steps to make amends. Few days ago, I had to call my family together and apologize to everyone. I believe that sometimes I may have tried to act overly with exercising authority and even do it to the unhappiness of others. I discovered that most times when I'm broke I'm often irritated and allow this irritation to burn towards others, especially my wife and immediate family members. So I did have to say sorry to every one of them.

"Don't be too proud to call your family members together and say, "I am sorry. I've not treated all of you well in the past. I've allowed anger to make me say things I ought not to have to said to you all. Please everyone, forgive me."

"It doesn't reduce you, rather it adds to you. As a woman

don't be too proud to say to your husband and family (children and house assistants) "I am sorry. I messed up. Forgive me everyone."

"As a leader or manager don't be too proud to make amends with your juniors. Saying I am sorry doesn't make you smaller than anyone. It is not saying sorry that actually makes you small and closes your doors.

"Those you owe, call them and say sorry. Start making plans to repay them. Look deep inside yourself and desire to make amends with anyone or group of persons that your actions of ignorance may have hurt in the past.

"Make Forgiveness your lifestyle and let God bring His plans to pass in your life."

Direction

Begin your prayer session with worship, thanksgiving to

God and praise to His Holy name. This empowers you and your environment for the manifestation of God's power.

Read the Following Scriptures

- Mark 11:25,

- Matthew 6:14-15,

- Matthew 18:21-22,

- James 5:16,

- Luke 6:27

- Colossians 3:13,

- 1 Corinthians 10:13,

- Psalms 103:10-14.

Prayers

1. Dear Heavenly Father,

I thank You for Your gift of forgiveness. Your only begotten Son, Jesus Christ, loved me enough to come to this world and experience the worst pain imaginable so I could be forgiven. I thank You for Your Love and kindness flows to me in spite of my errors and mistakes. Be praised forever and ever, in Jesus name.

2. O LORD, I pray this day that You clothe me with Your unconditional LOVE in perfect harmony of the Spirit according to Colossians 3:14. Help me to develop unconditional love from this day forward, even to those who have offended and hurt me in the past and those who will try to provoke me in the future, in Jesus name.

---

3. Father LORD, to be fair, I feel scarred most times when I'm hurt and offended. I feel betrayed and letdown. In fact, I feel very bad sometimes.

But I pray today LORD, may Your gentle WORDS saturate my mind and direct my thoughts. Help me to release the hurt I feel and start to LOVE as Jesus Christ loves.

Help me to see my offender through our Savior's eyes. Help me to continue to pray and stand in the gap for the salvation of their souls. I believe that if I can be forgiven, so can they. I therefore pray that You touch their hearts and bring them unto salvation, for it is not your will that any should perish.

In Jesus name I pray.

---

4. O LORD, Let Your peace that passes understanding saturate my heart. Let Your peace rule my thoughts, emotions and imaginations, and keep away doubts, fears and questions from me permanently.

As I declare that I forgive in words, May the Holy Spirit fill my heart with peace and truly make me to forgive.

LORD, at any time that I see the person who hurt me, bring this prayer back to my remembrance, so I can take any ungodly thoughts captive and make them obedient to Christ. (2 Cor. 10:5) And may the confidence of Christ in my heart guide me into the freedom of forgiveness. I praise you for the work you are doing in my life, teaching and perfecting my faith.

In Jesus' Name.

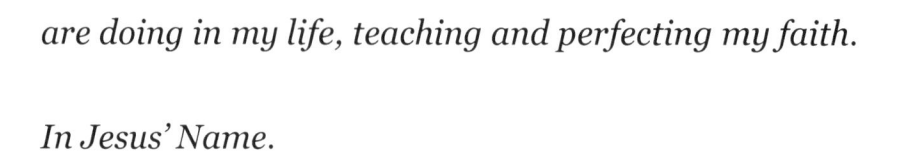

5. *"Heavenly Father, I pray this day that the root, seeds, and branches of unforgivenes and bitterness be rooted out of my life, in Jesus name.*

---

6. *From this day O LORD, I declare that I hold nothing against anyone. I forgive everyone and receive my deliverance and healing from anger, in Jesus' name.*

---

7. *Today O LORD, I release these ones who I have something against (Mention names that you remember).*

LORD, I pray that You forgive and bless them.

In Jesus name.

---

8. Heavenly Father, I thank You for the grace and power that you have now bestowed on me to walk in forgiveness and bear fruit for Your Kingdom here on earth. Be praised forever and ever, in Jesus name.

Prayer 3: Surrender Your Right to Be Angry

"But more than that, I count everything as loss compared to the priceless privilege and supreme advantage of knowing Christ Jesus my Lord [and of growing more deeply and thoroughly acquainted with Him—a joy unequaled]. ***For His sake I have lost everything, and I consider it all garbage, so that I may gain Christ.****"*

- Philippians 3:8 (AMP)

There are situations and times when it is right for one to get angry. Just as we're praying to be set free from anger, such situations will still come in the future. For example, when you have done your best to assist somebody and the person ignores you, refuses to appreciate your efforts, or even undermines and insults you in the public. No doubt, if you get angry, you may have some justification. But God wants you to surrender this right to Him.

I was told about a man of God who has labored in a church for over 30 years. Just as it got closer to when he would retire, the senior pastor's wife connived with a few others and roped the man into a situation where he was suspended from the ministry, found himself being investigated for fraud, immorality and all what not. In situations like this, this man of God has a right to be angry. But Apostle Paul is saying that we must be willing to lay our rights down just so we can gain Christ.

Laying this right down before God means we are surrendering to God to carry out vengeance for us. It means we are withdrawing from our rights to retaliate, either in words or actions. As we lay this right down before God, we can be rest assured that justice will prevail, because God is a God of justice.

Direction

Begin your prayer session with worship, thanksgiving to God and praise to His Holy name. This empowers you and your environment for the manifestation of God's power.

Read the Following Scriptures

Proverbs 3:5 - 3:6 - Trust in the LORD with all thine heart; and lean not unto thine own understanding. In all thy ways acknowledge him, and he shall direct thy paths.

1 Corinthians 10:13 - There hath no temptation taken you but such as is common to man: but God [is] faithful, who will not suffer you to be tempted above that ye are able; but will with the temptation also make a way to escape, that ye may be able to bear [it].

Matthew 16:24-25 - Then Jesus said to His disciples, "If anyone wishes to come after Me, he must deny himself, and take up his cross and follow Me. "For whoever wishes to save his life will lose it; but whoever loses his life for My sake will find it.

Romans 12:1 (AMP) - Therefore I urge you, brothers and sisters, by the mercies of God, to present your bodies [dedicating all of yourselves, set apart] as a living sacrifice, holy and well-pleasing to God, which is your rational (logical, intelligent) act of worship.

Prayers

1. Precious Father, I present my body to You as a living sacrifice. Make it holy and pleasing to Thee. I present my mind, thoughts and emotions to Thee. Sanctify me wholly unto Thee. From this day forward, LORD, May I become an acceptable instrument of worship to Thee, in my spirit, soul and body.

In Jesus name

---

2. LORD Jesus, I desire to follow Thee. I know that no cross is too much for me bear because of You. I know that You will not allow me to be tempted beyond what I can bear. So, LORD, I surrender my rights to Thee.

Today and every day LORD, I surrender my rights to become angry and take vengeance to You.

When I'm tempted in the future to become angry, please remind me of this prayer by the Holy Spirit, and afterwards give me the grace to continue to surrender this right to Thee.

In Jesus name.

3. O LORD, I hereby declare my trust in Thee with all mine heart. May I learn not to lean and depend on my own understanding henceforth.

Teach me and remind me how to acknowledge Thee in all situations, even in situations of provocation. At such moments of weakness, guide me and help me, according to Thy WORD, to learn to say and do the right things.

In Jesus Name.

---

4. Dear Father, I make an unconditional surrender of every aspect of my life to Your loving care and control today. Please give me your strength and wisdom and peace and purpose.

You know how I have resented the challenges in my

life, and you know how I have battled the things that have caused me pain that I can't change. You know that I've asked you many times for an explanation that has never come.

Today, I want to stop fighting you over things I don't understand. Help me to change the things that I can, and help me to accept the things that cannot be changed.

Help me to trust in Your love and care when things don't make sense.

Help me to trust that you are a good God and that you have my best interest at heart.

I Jesus Name

---

5. Thank You Everlasting Father, for accepting and answering my prayers, in Jesus name.

Prayer 4: Bind the Spirit of Anger

"Put on all of God's armor so that you will be able to stand safe against all strategies and tricks of Satan. 12 For we are not fighting against people made of flesh and blood, but against persons without bodies—the evil rulers of the unseen world, those mighty satanic beings and great evil princes of darkness who rule this world; and against huge numbers of wicked spirits in the spirit world."

- Ephesians 6:11-12 (TLB)

Like I said, anger is spiritual. But as a child of God, you have power to bind and cast out this spirit of anger and its associated demons out of your life and home. You have power to claim your complete freedom in Christ Jesus. If you don't rise and claim your deliverance, the demon will continue to attack you. So that is what we are going to do today.

Scriptures for Meditation

James 4:7 - "Submit yourselves to God. Resist the devil, and he will flee from you."

2 Cor. 10:3-5 - "For though we live in the world, we do not wage war as the world does. The weapons we fight with are not the weapons of the world. On the contrary, they have divine power to demolish strongholds. We demolish arguments and every pretension that sets itself up against the knowledge of God, and we take captive every thought to make it obedient to Christ."

1 Pet. 5:8-9 - "Be self-controlled and alert. Your enemy the devil prowls around like a roaring lion looking for someone to devour. *Resist him, standing firm in the faith."*

Isaiah 54:17 - "No weapon that is formed against you will prosper; and every tongue that accuses you in judgment you will condemn. This is the heritage of the servants of the Lord, and their vindication is from Me," declares the Lord."

1 Cor. 15:57 - "But thanks be to God, who gives us the victory through our Lord Jesus Christ."

Matt. 18:18-19 - "Truly I tell you, whatever you bind on earth will be bound in heaven, and whatever you loose on earth will be loosed in heaven. Again, truly I tell you that if two of you on earth agree about anything they ask for, it will be done for them by my Father in heaven."

1 John 4:4 - "You are from God, little children, and

have overcome them; because greater is He who is in you than he who is in the world."

2 Thess. 3:3 - "But the Lord is faithful, and he will strengthen you and protect you from the evil one."

Luke 10:19 - "Behold, I have given you authority to tread on serpents and scorpions, and over all the power of the enemy, and nothing shall hurt you."

Psalm 91:1-4 - "He who dwells in the shelter of the Most High will rest in the shadow of the Almighty. I will say of the Lord, He is my refuge and my fortress, my God, in whom I trust. Surely he will save you from the fowler's snare and from the deadly pestilence. He will cover you with his feathers, and under his wings you will find refuge; his faithfulness will be your shield and rampart…"

2 Chron. 20:15 - "This is what the Lord says to you:

'Do not be afraid or discouraged because of this vast army. For the battle is not yours, but God's."

Direction

Begin your prayer session with worship, thanksgiving to God and praise to His Holy name. This empowers you and your environment for the manifestation of God's power.

Prayers

1. Father in heaven, In the name of Jesus Christ, I come before You this day once again and plead the Blood of Jesus Christ over my spirit, soul and body.

By the Blood of Jesus I receive forgiveness of sins and re-union with You. I am a new creature in Christ Jesus and old things have passed away. I am Your workmanship, recreated in Christ as a priest and king to reign here on earth.

2. *O LORD, According to Your Word, I am joined to Christ in one Spirit (I cor. 6:17) and so cannot be joined to any other spirit. I therefore plead my case this day and declare that anger spirit have no ground to be connected to my spirit, soul and body henceforth, in Jesus name.*

3. *Heavenly Father, As I intercede and pray this day, I surrender myself to the Holy Spirit and ask that You bring to my attention anything that is serving as an opening in my life for the spirits of anger, feud, frustration, revenge and rage to attack me.*

Show me areas of my life that needs to be attended to and objects or materials that are with me that I need to destroy, in Jesus name.

4. O LORD, You said in Isaiah 49: 25 that You will fight against those that fight against me and save me and my children.

I therefore hand over this battle against the spirits of anger over to You in faith and declare that I have victory already, in Jesus name.

---

5. Jesus Christ was made manifest that He might destroy all the works of the devil. So every work of the devil in my life and family are hereby declared to go into a destruction mode.

I hold in my hand the victory Jesus Christ purchased on the cross of Calvary, when He made an open show of principalities and powers and triumphed over them.

I take my position in Christ as one given power to

become a child of God, even joint heir with Christ to execute judgment against every form of disobedience exhibited against the knowledge of God in my life and family, in Jesus name.

---

6. *I come against the evil strongholds of anger, feud and rage against my life and family. I command them to be destroyed right now, in Jesus name.*

---

7. *I take authority over the strong hold of ANGER and I command all demons in this stronghold to leave me now based on the finished work of Christ on the CROSS, In Jesus name.*

---

8. *You king spirit of anger in my life, I bind you with chains of fire in Jesus name. (Ps. 149.7-9)*

9. *Every noble spirits associated with anger: abandonment, feuding, frustration, hatred, murder, punishment, rage, wrath, resentment, in my life, I bind you with fetters of iron, and I cast you spirits out right now and send you all to hell, in Jesus name.*

10. *O LORD, let every door opened in my life by the spirit of anger, be closed this day, in Jesus name.*

11. *O LORD, I pollute every demonic kingdom from where attacks are being coordinated against my life and family by the Blood of Jesus Christ. I overrun every demonic queen or king enthroned against my life and family, and I trample on all the snakes and scorpions being used against me from the spirit world,*

in Jesus name.

---

12. Today, I declare again, Jesus is the only LORD and Savior of my life. He is the only King and husband of my life.

So no you evil queens, kings, princes and princesses from the rivers and coasts, working against my life and my destiny, hear the WORD of God...You have no ground to claim connection with me henceforth. I therefore bind you all and command you to get back into the abyss in Jesus name.

---

13. It is written in Acts 17:30 that in the days of Ignorance the LORD has overlooked. Whatever I have done in the past that became a ground for evil spirits of anger to claim connection to me is hereby erased by the

Blood of Jesus Christ.

---

14. Whatever evil instrument in my possession, knowingly or unknowingly, I command them to be exposed and destroyed by fire this day, in Jesus name.

---

15. Any witchcraft practice against my life, receive immediate judgment of fire this day, in the name of Jesus Christ.

---

16. I destroy any demonic instrument being used to monitor and remote control my life and destiny, in Jesus name.

---

17. Every agent of the devil physically attached to my life, home and marriage, to frustrate me, be exposed and decease by fire from now onwards, in Jesus name.

---

18. Today, LORD, *I reverse and nullify every form of bewitchments, enchantments, curses, spells and divinations against me, in the name of Jesus Christ.*

---

21. *Wherever meetings have been held or are holding or will be held against me by demons and witches, I attack such gatherings with God's WORD in Isaiah 54:15, which says that they shall gather together but their gathering is not of the LORD and whoever gathers against me shall fall.*

I command every demonic gathering of witches and marine spirits in the marine world against me to scatter by fire, in Jesus name.

---

19. *From this day forward, I render all evil decisions and decrees taken against my life and destiny to nothing, in Jesus name.*

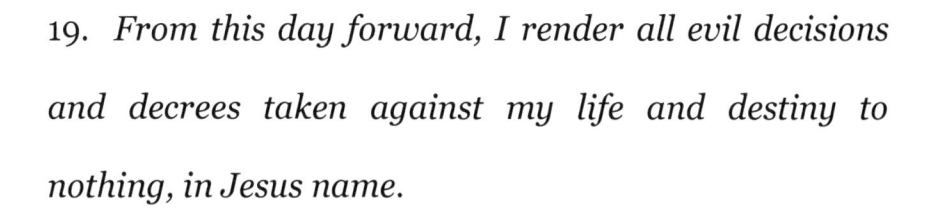

20. *I command every demon released to monitor my life and activate demonic decisions to collapse and become blind this moment, and be bundled into the abyss by fire, in Jesus name.*

---

21. *Every familiar spirits from my village, place of my birth or generational lineage, attached to my spirit, my home, my destiny, in any way, I bind you all right now, I cast you all into abyss, in the name of Jesus Christ.*

---

22. *This day, I declare with God's Word in Isaiah 60:4-6 and say:*

My blessings and prosperity shall gather together and come to me.

I will carry my sons and daughters and grandchildren.

I will be radiant and my heart shall be filled with joy from now onwards.

Riches and wealth and the abundance of the sea shall be turned to me.

The wealth of the nations shall come to me.

Men and women will bring gold and frankincense and submit them to my feet.

And my mouth shall be filled with good news, in Jesus name.

---

23. I decree according to 1 Peter 2:24 that Jesus carried my sins and diseases and pains at the cross. By

His wounds I am healed.

Every sickness and affliction in my body is a stranger. And from today, they have no more place in my life and family. Therefore, you afflictions and pains in my life and family caused by spirits of anger and witchcraft, cease right now in Jesus name.

---

24. Thank You LORD Jesus Christ for my deliverance and permanent victory over the spirit of anger and the kingdom of darkness and their operations.

There shall be no reinforcement or evil reunion against me henceforth, for afflictions shall not rise a second time (Nahum 1:9)

I seal my victory and confessions with the blood of Jesus and I cover myself with the blood of Jesus.

In Jesus name.

Prayer 5: Manifesting the Fruits of the Holy Spirit

"But the fruit of the Spirit [the result of His presence within us] is love [unselfish concern for others], joy, [inner] peace, patience [not the ability to wait, but how we act while waiting], kindness, goodness, faithfulness, gentleness, self-control. Against such things there is no law."

- Galatians 5:22-23 (AMP)

Anger and its related weaknesses are also regarded as works of the flesh, that is, fruits of earthly nature. And the remedy for these works of the flesh is bearing fruits of the Spirit. As we pray and uproot the seeds of the flesh in us, we can ask the Holy Spirit to replace each of these fleshly fruits with fruits of the Spirit.

Do not get it wrong. These fruits of the Spirit take time to grow and develop in us. Just as the Bible rightly says, they are FRUITS; and fruits do take some time to mature. As we rightly desire, pray, seek the LORD, study the WORD, and worship, we create the right atmosphere for these fruits to be developed in us.

Scriptures for Meditation

John 15:1-8:

"I am the true vine, and My Father is the vinedresser. "Every branch in Me that does not bear fruit, He takes away; and every branch that bears fruit, He prunes it so that it may bear more fruit. "You are already clean because of the word which I have spoken to you.

"Abide in Me, and I in you. As the branch cannot bear fruit of itself unless it abides in the vine, so neither can you unless you abide in Me. "I am the vine, you are the branches; he who abides in Me and I in him, he bears much fruit, for apart from Me you can do nothing. "

If anyone does not abide in Me, he is thrown away as a branch and dries up; and they gather them, and cast them into the fire and they are burned.

"If you abide in Me, and My words abide in you, ask whatever you wish, and it will be done for you."My Father is glorified by this, that you bear much fruit, and so prove to be My disciples.

Ephesians 5:8-11:

For you were formerly darkness, but now you are Light in the Lord; walk as children of Light (for the fruit of the Light consists in all goodness and righteousness and truth), trying to learn what is pleasing to the Lord. Do not participate in the unfruitful deeds of darkness, but instead even expose them.

James 3:18:

And the seed whose fruit is righteousness is sown in peace by those who make peace.

Ephesians 4:2:

Be always humble, gentle, and patient. Show your love by being tolerant with one another.

Direction

Begin your prayer session with worship, thanksgiving to God and praise to His Holy name. This empowers you and your environment for the manifestation of God's power.

Prayers

1. Heavenly Father, Thank You for engrafting me in Christ Jesus by the Holy Spirit as a branch. You designed me to bear fruits of righteousness, love, peace, joy, gentleness, self-control, goodness, patience, and kindness.

O LORD, I desire to bear these fruits in my life henceforth. I therefore pray that You empower my heart to start and continue to bear these fruits

In Jesus name.

---

2. Dear Holy Spirit, I desire to remain rooted in Christ, bearing fruits that lead others to the light of God's love.

I desire to walk in LOVE, forgiving others at all times and gifting God's blessings in my life with others, just as God Loved and gave Jesus to die for us.

I desire to walk in joy every day of my life, thereby drawing from the well of salvation.

Please remind and help me at all times to LOVE and be joyful as I live, in Jesus name.

---

3. Dear Holy Spirit, I desire to walk in peace with myself and with others as a child of God. I desire to walk in patience, for faith makes no haste.

I desire to walk in kindness, thoughtfulness and compassion for others just as Christ was compassionate at all times.

Provide me with daily assistance to bear these fruits of peace, patience and kindness in abundance, so that Jesus will be glorified in my life every day, in Jesus name.

4. Dear Holy Spirit, I desire to bear the fruit of Goodness, so that I may lead others to Jesus Christ. I desire to be faithful at all times with whatever God blesses me with, so that I may stand before God in the end and receive the rewards of faithfulness.

I desire to be gentle with myself and others, in thoughts, words and actions, so that I may be an instrument of encouragement and uplifting to others and not discouragement.

I desire to walk in Self-control in food, dressing, and in everything so that I could win the race set before me and not be a cast away after preaching to others.

I call upon You to empower me every day to bear these fruits as I live, serve God and relate with others.

In Jesus name I pray. Amen.

Prayer 6: Prayer for Those Who Struggle With Anger

When we pray for others, our own hurts are healed. That is the principle of sowing and reaping. As you earnestly and honestly pray for those you know who are struggling with anger, God's power is released to reach out to them, and also to you. This could be your loved ones, spouse, colleagues, etc.

Here's an example of prayer for someone you know battling with anger sent in by a reader, Lee:

"Heavenly Father,

I pray that You help my husband with his violent temper. I forgive him and I ask that you forgive him. And even now that we are apart...wherever he is please protect him and deliver him from all forms of evil and wickedness. Show him Your unfailing love and mercy.

Grant him grace to come to you in repentance. Help him make his relationship with You right and stronger, that he will fall in love with You and Your Word again. Remove any and everything that hinders him from seeing You clearly. In Jesus name"

As you spend time to genuinely pray for others, God not only visits those you pray for, He also visits and blesses you abundantly. I encourage you to start from today to pray earnestly for others welfare, deliverance and salvation. Go to God in humility and sincerely pray for persons in your life held by one form of stronghold or the other, like anger, etc.

I'm not talking about some general prayers of, *"LORD, save these people in this community."* No. I'm taking about making a list names of few persons on paper and pray for their genuine salvation. The Bible says:

I tell you that in the same way there will be more rejoicing in heaven over one sinner who repents than over ninety-nine righteous persons who do not need to repent. – Luke 15:7

As you join to create joy in heaven by genuinely praying for the salvation of others, God moves into your life and destroys whatever is causing you pain and sorrow, whatever they are.

Scriptures for Reflection

Matthew 18:14– "Even so it is not the will of your Father who is in heaven that one of these little ones should perish."

2 Peter 3:9 – "The Lord is not slack concerning His promise, as some count slackness, but is longsuffering toward us, not willing that any should perish but that all should come to repentance."

1 Timothy 2:3-4 – "This is good, and pleases God our Savior, who wants all people to be saved and to come to a knowledge of the truth."

Acts 16:31 – "Believe in the Lord Jesus and you will be saved, along with everyone in your household."

Luke 11:5-10 – Then Jesus said to them, "Suppose you have a friend, and you go to him at midnight and say, 'Friend, lend me three loaves of bread; a friend of mine on a journey has come to me, and I have no food to offer him.'

And suppose the one inside answers, 'Don't bother me. The door is already locked, and my children and I are in bed. I can't get up and give you anything.'

I tell you, even though he will not get up and give you the bread because of friendship, yet because of your shameless audacity[a] he will surely get up and give you as much as you need.

"So I say to you: Ask and it will be given to you; seek and you will find; knock and the door will be opened to you.

For everyone who asks receives; the one who seeks finds; and to the one who knocks, the door will be opened.

Direction

Begin your prayer session with worship, thanksgiving to God and praise to His Holy name. This empowers you and your environment for the manifestation of God's power.

Please replace the dots with the names of the persons you are praying for.

Prayers

1. O LORD, I Thank You because You do not want me,

my family, my children and these people I have here on my list to perish. Thank you LORD because You want us all to be saved. This is the assurance I have in YOU that as I pray, I receive answers. In Jesus name.

---

2. Today O LORD, I declare that these ones shall be saved and come the knowledge of the truth in Christ Jesus. I declare that they will be set free from anger, pain, feud and every stronghold that is holding them bound, in Jesus name.

---

3. Father I pray this day, Let Your power of salvation visit them. O LORD, visit ————————wherever they are right now. Visit them in the name of Jesus Christ.

---

4. Father LORD, I ask that out of Your unlimited

resources You will empower ————————— with inner strength to accept Jesus as their LORD and Savior. In Jesus name.

---

5. Cause .... to be planted deep in the Love of Christ. Let them be rooted deep in Your love and comprehend with all of God's people the extravagant dimensions of Your love. In Jesus name.

---

6. I come against the spirit of rebellion, anger, feud, unforgiveness, immorality and hate in the life of ——— ——-in Jesus name. I cast out these spirits and every spirit of stubbornness; I command these anti-salvation spirits to be drowned in the abyss in the Mighty name of Jesus Christ.

7. Satan, I command you right now to lose your grips on ———————-in Jesus name.

---

8. Jesus sets you—————— free, you are therefore free indeed. You are no longer under the influence of anger, Satan and sin. In Jesus name.

---

9. Wherever you are—————— Receive encounter with Jesus right now. In Jesus Name.

---

10. Because you ———————- are connected to me and I believe in Christ and His Love, you are saved from sin to serve the living God through Christ Jesus. In Jesus name.

Thank You LORD Jesus for setting……………………..free to serve You forever.

Prayer 7: Declare the Promises of God For Your Life and Family

"For the word of God [is] quick, and powerful, and sharper than any two edged sword, piercing even to the dividing asunder of soul and spirit, and of the joints and marrow, and [is] a discerner of the thoughts and intents of the heart."

- Hebrews 4:12

NOTE: All the prayers and declarations below are culled from the book, <u>Prayers for the Year</u>, by Daniel C. Okpara

The Word of God is powerful enough to create the

realities of God in your life and destiny. Start declaring the promises of God about your health, emotions and life.

Take out time today to go through these powerful prayer declarations. Copy them out and try to personalize some to yourself after this season. God said to Joshua, "This book of the law shall not depart out of thy mouth; but thou shalt meditate therein day and night, that thou mayest observe to do according to all that is written therein: for then thou shalt make thy way prosperous, and then thou shalt have good success." (Joshua 1:8).

Declaration 1: I Am God's Workmanship

PROMISE:

"For we are God's handiwork, created in Christ Jesus to do good works, which God prepared in advance for us to do." - Ephesians 2:10

DECLARATION:

"I am God's design, created in Christ Jesus, reborn from above, spiritually transformed and renewed, doing good works, which God prepared for me beforehand.

I am living the good life, which He prearranged and made ready for me.

"I am walking in the Light; darkness has no place in me.

"I am shinning day by day, fulfilling the plans of God for my life, in Jesus name."

Declaration 2: God's Plans for Me

PROMISE:

"For I know the plans I have for you," declares the Lord, "plans to prosper you and not to harm you, plans to give you hope and a future." - Jeremiah 29:11

DECLARATION:

"The plan of God for my life is peace, health and prosperity. When I pray, I have confidence that God answers my prayers.

My future is safe and secure.

I have no need to fear and worry about life and what it brings, for God is working out everything for my good.

In Jesus name."

Declaration 3: **I Am The Light Of The World.**

PROMISE:

"You are the light of the world. A city on a hill cannot be hidden. Neither do people light a lamp and put it under a basket. Instead, they set it on a lampstand, and it gives light to everyone in the house." – **Matthew 5:14-15**

DECLARATION:

I am a light of Christ to the world. A city set on a hill which cannot be hidden. I am an example and a testimony to the world.

My light is shining every day, towards the perfect day.

I am excelling and winning in all that I do.

In Jesus name. Amen

Declaration 4: **Divine Health Is Mine**

PROMISE:

"Praise the Lord, my soul, and forget not all his benefits— who forgives all our sins and heals all your diseases, who redeems your life from the pit and crowns you with love and compassion." - Psalm 103:2-4

DECLARATION:

"My body is God's temple. No sickness and disease is permitted in my body.

The death of Jesus on the cross brings me total healing. Daily, I am walking in divine health.

I have emotional peace. I have physical health and I have spiritual strength. I am strong in every area of my life, in Jesus name.

Declaration 5: **Free From Condemnation**

PROMISE:

"Therefore, there is now no condemnation for those who are in Christ Jesus, 2 because through Christ Jesus the law of the Spirit who gives life has set you free from the law of sin and death." - Romans 8:1-2

DECLARATION:

"I am free from condemnation, self-pity and self-judgment. I will not regret my past mistakes and failures, for all are recreated in Christ Jesus for my glory.

I am set free by the Almighty God through Christ Jesus. I am not righteous by my own works, but by the power of the Holy Spirit. Even though I have made grave mistakes in the past, God has forgiven me by the Blood of Jesus. No one can condemn me going forward, in Jesus name.

Declaration 6: Everything Works For My Good

PROMISE:

"And we know that in all things God works for the good of those who love him, who have been called according to his purpose." - Romans 8:28

DECLARATION:

"The minds and hearts of men are in the hand of God, and He turns them wherever He pleases, just like the rivers of water. I therefore declare that men and women are working for my good, spiritually, physically and in all circumstances.

I have favour with men and women, kings and princes, in all places. Everything and every person is working for my own good henceforth, in Jesus name.

Declaration 7: I Can Do All Things Through Christ

PROMISE:

"I can do all this through him who gives me strength." - Philippians 4:13

DECLARATION:

"I have the life of God in me. I have His wisdom and strength working on the inside of me. Therefore I can do all things through Christ who supports me.

I have understanding, strength and divine direction. I am not a confused fellow overwhelmed with life and circumstances.

I am in complete control of my life and everything that comes my way, for the Holy Spirit, my Senior Partner, will always guide me on what to do and how to proceed.

By the Holy Spirit, I will always know what to do, when to do it and how to do it, at all times and in all circumstances.

In Jesus name.

Other Books from The Same Authors

1. Prayer Retreat: 21 Days Devotional With 500 Powerful Prayers & Declarations to Destroy Stubborn Demonic Problems, Dislodge Every Spiritual Wickedness Against Your Life and Release Your Detained Blessings

2. HEALING PRAYERS & CONFESSIONS: Powerful Daily Meditations, Prayers and Declarations for Total Healing and Divine Health.

3. 200 Violent Prayers for Deliverance, Healing and Financial Breakthrough.

4. Hearing God's Voice in Painful Moments: 21 Days Bible Meditations and Prayers to Bring Comfort, Strength and Healing When Grieving for the Loss of Someone You Love.

5. Healing Prayers: 30 Powerful Prophetic Prayers that Brings Healing and Empower You to Walk in Divine Health.

6. Healing WORDS: 55 Powerful Daily Confessions &

Declarations to Activate Your Healing & Walk in Divine Health: Strong Decrees That Invoke Healing for You & Your Loved Ones

7. Prayers That Break Curses and Spells and Release Favors and Breakthroughs.

8. 7 Days Fasting With 120 Powerful Night Prayers for Personal Deliverance and Breakthrough.

9. 100 Powerful Prayers for Your Teenagers: Powerful Promises and Prayers to Let God Take Control of Your Teenagers & Get Them to Experience Love & Fulfillment

10. How to Pray for Your Children Everyday: + 75 Powerful Prayers & Prophetic Declarations to Use and Pray for Your Children's Salvation, Future, Health, Education, Career, Relationship, Protection, etc

11. How to Pray for Your Family: + 70 Powerful Prayers and Prophetic Declarations for Your Family's Salvation, Healing, Victory, Breakthrough & Total Restoration.

12. <u>Daily Prayer Guide:</u> A Practical Guide to Praying and Getting Results – Learn How to Develop a Powerful Personal Prayer Life

13. <u>Make Him Respect You:</u> 31 Relationship Advice for Women to Make their Men Respect Them.

14. <u>How to Cast Out Demons from Your Home, Office and Property:</u> 100 Powerful Prayers to Cleanse Your Home, Office, Land & Property from Demonic Attacks

15. <u>Praying Through the Book of Psalms:</u> Most Powerful Psalms and Powerful Prayers & Declarations for Every Situation: Birthday, Christmas, Business Ideas, Breakthrough, Deliverance, Healing, Comfort, Exams, Decision Making, Grief, and Many More.

16. <u>STUDENTS' PRAYER BOOK:</u> Powerful Motivation & Guide for Students & Anyone Preparing to Write Exams: Plus 10 Days of Powerful Prayers for Wisdom, Favor, Protection & Success in Studies, Exams & Life.

17. How to Pray and Receive Financial Miracle: Powerful Prayers for Financial Miracles, Business and Career Breakthrough

18. Prayers to Destroy Witchcraft Attacks Against Your Life & Family and Release Your Blessings

19. Deliverance from Marine Spirits: Powerful Prayers to Overcome Marine Spirits – Spirit Husbands and Spirit Wives – Permanently

20. Deliverance From Python Spirit: Powerful Prayers to Defeat the Python Spirit – Spirit of Lies, Deceptions and Oppression.

Contact Us

We love testimonies. We love to hear what God is doing around the world as people draw close to Him in prayer. Please share your story with us.

Also, please consider giving this book a review on Amazon and checking out our other titles at: www.amazon.com/author/danielokpara .

I also invite you to checkout our website at www.BetterLifeWorld.org and consider joining our newsletter, which we send out once in a while with great tips, testimonies and revelations from God's Word for a victorious living.

Feel free to drop us your prayer request. We will join faith with you and God's power will be released in your life and the issue in question.

About the Author.

Daniel Chika Okpara is a husband, father, pastor, businessman and lecturer. He is the author and publisher of the popular daily devotional, "MOVING FORWARD." He has authored over 50 life transforming books on business, prayer, relationship and victorious living.

He is the president of Better Life World Outreach Centre - www.betterlifeworld.org - a non-denominational evangelism ministry committed to global prayer revival and evangelism.

Through the monthly Better Life Crusades, Better Life Health and Business Breakthrough Seminars and Better Life

TV, thousands of lives have been won to the LORD, healed, blessed and restored to a purposeful living.

He holds a Master's Degree in Theology from Cornerstone Christian University and is married to Prophetess Doris Okpara, his prayer warrior, best friend and biggest support in life. They are blessed with two lovely kids (Isaac and Annabel).

If you are looking to connect with someone who understands the challenges and issues of life and is willing to pray with you, provide counseling and believe God for a way forward then Daniel Okpara is your man. You can connect with him at www.betterlifeworld.org for prayers and counseling.